AFRICAN-AMERICAN ARTS

DANCE

Angela Shelf Medearis and Michael R. Medearis

Twenty-First Century Books
A Division of Henry Holt and Company • New York

Twenty-First Century Books
A Division of Henry Holt and Company, Inc.
115 West 18th Street
New York, NY 10011

Henry Holt® and colophon are trademarks of
Henry Holt and Company, Inc.
Publishers since 1866

Published in Canada by Fitzhenry & Whiteside Ltd.
195 Allstate Parkway, Markham, Ontario, L3R 4T8

Library of Congress Cataloging-in-Publication Data
Medearis, Angela Shelf
Dance / Angela S. Medearis, Michael R. Medearis.
p. cm.—(African-American arts)
Includes bibliographical references (p.) and index.
Summary: Explores the dance traditions of African Americans, from
their origins in the expressive dances that the slaves brought from Africa
through the development of jazz and tap to modern dance and ballet.
1. Afro-American dance—History—Juvenile literature. 2. Dance, Black—History—
Juvenile literature. 3. Dancers—United States—Juvenile literature. [1. Afro-American dance—
History. 2. Dance—History.] I. Medearis, Michael. II. Title. III. Series.
GV1624.7.A34M33 1997
793.3' 1973—DC21   96-45198
                                                                                              CIP
                                                                                              AC

ISBN 0-8050-4481-7
First Edition—1997

DESIGNED BY KELLY SOONG

Printed in the United States of America
All first editions are printed on acid-free paper. ∞

1 3 5 7 9 10 8 6 4 2

Photo credits
p. 4 (top): © M. & E. Bernheim/Woodfin Camp; pp. 4 (bottom), 61, 63, 72: © Jack Vartoogian; p. 7:
© Betty Press/Woodfin Camp; pp. 8, 16: Corbis/Bettmann; p. 11: © Roger-Viollet/Gamma Liaison;
pp. 13, 21, 22: The Granger Collection; p. 17: © Stock Montage, Inc.; p. 18: Schomberg Center for
Research in Black Culture; p. 25: Mary Evans Picture Library; p. 29: Brown Brothers; pp. 31, 38, 49, 68:
© Archive Photos; pp. 33, 43, 53: UPI/Corbis-Bettmann; pp. 34, 45, 69: Photofest; p. 37: Peter Newark's
American Pictures; p. 41: Index Stock Photography PhotoLibrary; p. 56: Metropolitan Opera Archives; p.
59: © Jack Mitchell; p. 66: © Lester Sloan/Woodfin Camp; p. 75: © Dan Rest/Brooklyn Academy of Music.

CONTENTS

The heritage continues . . .

INTRODUCTION

In the West African country of Burkina Faso, a dancer moves his long mask through the air. Fluttering his arms like the wings of a butterfly, he swoops up, then down. He dances a ritual drama about the first heavy rains of the season called the Butterfly Dance.

Every festival celebrated in Africa has its own ritual of dance, music, and song. The ceremonies provide a sense of togetherness and shared values within the village. Each dance is a drama that sometimes starts in a closely knit circle. All attention is on the dancers, who wear elaborately painted masks or body paint. Their story unfolds with intricate steps and spontaneous movements. Their arms spiral and their legs and torsos move freely in a style that is called multiunit.

In West Africa, dance is used in symbolic rituals of everyday life. Dances are performed as part of celebrations, initiation rites for the young boys and girls of the tribe, special tribal festivals, and some religious rituals. A dance may celebrate a birth or honor a death.

Sometimes a dance becomes wild and frenzied in a style called convulsive dancing. For example, a witch doctor or medicine man may lead a dance to cure a sick person. The person is placed in the center of the dance circle. The dancers elevate themselves into a state of ecstasy and then collapse.

The people in the community not only watch a dance but also often join in to become a part of the presentation. The ones who began the dance may take their performance out of their circle and into the audience.

Anyone who has ever enjoyed the art of dance has experienced the contributions of African Americans to this art form. Many exciting varieties of modern dance have come from African Americans. These dances are known throughout the world for their high energy, artistic improvisation, and uniquely creative forms of movement. Much of modern American dance has been directly or indirectly influenced by African cultural dance traditions.

The European dance tradition was brought to America by the early colonists. European dancing was often a single-unit or harmonic style. The torso is held stiff and straight, and there is little arm movement and almost no spontaneous actions. Dancers moved in orderly groups to a set pattern of steps. Europeans used dance to enhance social activities and as a means of physical recreation and entertainment. Dance was not viewed as a form of expression.

In Africa, dance was the language that wove a vital thread through the social and cultural fabric of the people. It served as a link between people, the earth, and the spiritual forces that were believed to influence all natural and human events. Dance was an expression of freedom and power.

In West African culture, music, song, and dance helped to identify each individual's role within a group and a group's role within the community. Power and honor were bestowed upon an *oba* (king) in Yorubaland (Nigeria) only when he was able to establish his authority by his expert performance of a formal traditional dance. As the ruler he was to lead the procession, dancing in a proud and dignified manner. His clothing, mannerisms, and movements expressed to the people his royal position in the tribe. The *oba* was followed by his wives, lesser chiefs, hunters, and other members of the community. Each person was identified by a dance appropriate to his or her status.

Dances in ancient West Africa were performed mostly as an important part of religious rituals in traditional ceremonies. An important aspect of African dances is that they were public events. All of the leaders of the tribes were expected to be skilled dancers before they were allowed to hold office. In traditional African society, the ability to dance was required of all physically able individuals. Dances in Africa today have a purpose that is more social than religious.

When Africans were taken from their homeland to become property in the slave trade of the New World, they were forced to accept a European-

A traditional African dance

based cultural tradition. Much of their reaction to slavery and the forced acceptance of a different culture came to be expressed in their dances. The repressive conditions of slavery caused many traditional dances to change forms.

European slave traders only partially understood the role of dance in the lives of their African captives. The traders made serious attempts to suppress the native dances performed by their African captives. These efforts produced some unexpected results. New dances were created, but they retained traits of the original African versions.

Native dances from Africa have left their mark on America's most popular social dances. In addition, the African-inspired improvisational aspects of jazz in dance music have been an important factor in the development of modern dance creations and performances in America and throughout the world.

The jitterbug was a popular dance in the 1930s and 1940s. Jitterbug steps and movements were often improvised.

It is impossible to separate modern dance from the music that goes with it. Both the music and the dances have their roots in Africa. The idea that dance should not be considered separately from its music is a foundation of African cultural philosophy. Social and concert dances in the United States have been subjected to African influences throughout their history. Early and modern American dance performances have also been affected by African-based movements and by African-American music such as spirituals, ragtime, blues, and jazz.

As we explore African dance traditions we will trace the beginnings of modern African-American and mainstream American-inspired dance forms.

ONE

THE MIDDLE PASSAGE—
DANCING THE SLAVES

During the seventeenth century, Africans were brought to the New World mainly from the countries of West Africa. For more than three hundred years, millions of African men, women, and children were captured for the slave trade. They were placed on extremely overcrowded ships staffed by European crews from England, Portugal, France, and the Netherlands. The journey across the Atlantic Ocean was the middle part of the long trip from Africa to the New World, so it was called the "middle passage."

From the time that African captives were taken on board the slave ships, the traders—slavers—treated them like animals. To have the largest amount of cargo possible, each captive was only allowed an average space of six feet by sixteen inches. The trip was long and dangerous. It could take from three to twelve weeks. Harsh weather and attacks by pirates or enemy ships were common.

The Africans were chained to each other while lying on their backs or their sides with little more than sixteen inches between them. Because of the chains, the captives were unable to stand or turn over without hurting themselves. Food rations were often insufficient and many captives starved. The crowded and unsanitary conditions caused the spread of diseases. Sometimes half of the captives died before the ship reached the Americas.

The slave ship captains wanted their captives to look healthy so they could sell them for higher prices in the New World. Once a day, weather permitting, the captives were brought on deck and were forced to do a cruel form of exercise that was referred to as "dancing the slaves."

The surgeon of the slave ship *Brookes* wrote the following eyewitness account of dancing the slaves in 1783:

> *After morning meals came a joyless ceremony called 'dancing the slaves.' Those who were in irons were ordered to stand up and make what motions they could, leaving a passage for such as were out of irons to dance around the deck.*

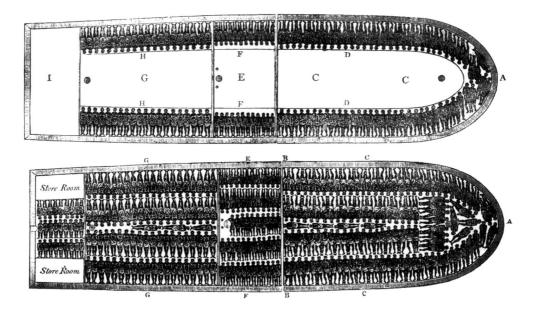

This drawing shows how tightly captives were packed into the hold of a slave ship.

Alexander Falconbridge was a surgeon on a slave ship in the mid to late 1700s. He gives us a view of the practice of dancing the slaves in his book *An Account of the Slave Trade on the Coast of Africa:*

> *Exercise being deemed necessary for the preservation of their health, they are sometimes obliged [forced] to dance, when the weather will permit their coming on deck. If they go about it reluctantly, or do not move with agility, they are flogged [whipped]; a person standing by them with a cat-o-nine-tails [whip with several leather strings] for that purpose. Their music, upon these occasions, consists of a drum. . . . The poor wretches are frequently compelled to sing also; but when they do so, their songs are generally, as may naturally be expected, melancholy lamentations [sad songs] of their exile from their native country.*

The African captives jumped up and down in their shackles; they rattled their chains; they turned and twisted. This movement was often done to the "music" of a broken drum, kettle, or upturned food pot. Such was the condition of the black people brought from Africa to the Americas.

The dance aboard slave ships was a sad experience for the African captives, who were used to experiencing dance as a joyous expression of freedom. They danced only because their captors wanted them to appear in good condition. It was not for love or joy, nor for religious or social celebration. They danced because they had to in order to survive. Dancing the slaves became so common that there were advertisements for musicians to play on board slave ships.

The slavers knew that dance was important to their captives and attempted to use dance as a tool to dominate them. But the slavers did not understand how powerful a force dance was in helping the captives to preserve and bring elements of their African culture to their new environment.

Dancing was believed to have a healing effect on the Africans. Some

*Captives were forced to dance on deck. This form of exercise
was supposed to keep them healthy on the long voyage.*

said that it would decrease diseases and keep the captives from committing suicide. It was commonly believed that if an African captive was not "amused and kept in motion, he would mope, squat down with his chin on his knees and arms clasped about his legs and in a very short time die." Dance exercise became one of the means by which the captives were kept alive during the horrible voyage from Africa to America.

Katherine Dunham, the great black choreographer and dance sociologist said in the foreword to Lynn Emery's book *Black Dance*, " . . . the dance by and large has been an instrument of black survival under the most depressing economic and social circumstances, and continues to be so."

T W O

AFRICAN DANCE
IN THE NEW WORLD

The power and beauty of African dancing and musical performances were observed by very few Europeans in Africa. European exposure to African dance was limited. Slave captain Theodore Canot described a group of African dancers in his journal:

> . . . a whirling circle of half-stripped girls [who] danced to the monotonous beat of a tom-tom. Presently, the formal ring was broken, and each female stepping out singly, danced to her individual fancy. Some were wild, some were soft, some were tame and some were fiery.

The brutal treatment of the captives was intended to make them cut all ties to their cultural traditions. These efforts of cultural repression were only partially successful. African dance traditions were too strong to be completely erased from the captives' memory. The African captives saved and passed on many of the basic elements of traditional African dance culture in spite of their harsh new environment.

The initial attitude of white people in the New World toward the rhythms and dances of recently arrived Africans depended mainly on the local situation. Protestant whites, who were in the majority, forced their African captives to accept their version of Christianity. Most people in the United States believed that Africans were less than human. Traditional African religions were not allowed.

African-based dance forms were not accepted by European or American society as a culturally significant art form for many years. The origins of this rejection go back to the early history of the United States. Rhythmic and expressive body movement in dance was criticized by the dominant English-based Protestant society as being corrupt and immoral. They believed that all forms of African dance were the product of a pagan, uncivilized, and backward culture. Although most of the early American settlers were uncomfortable with using the body as an expressive device in dance, they were secretly fascinated by the dances of their slaves.

In spite of the severe repression of native African dances, the slaves made changes to their dances while keeping some of the original African elements. The changes made the dances more acceptable to the slave owners. African dance was also affected by European dance forms, resulting in a cross-cultural mix that would become the basis of modern American social dancing.

The Spanish and French slaveholders believed that the expressions of African culture were examples of a primitive society. But the Spanish and French were more liberal than the English in their attitudes toward their African captives. This is the reason why more of the African cultural heritage in the Americas can be seen today in the states formerly dominated by the French and Spanish, such as Louisiana, Georgia, and South Carolina.

Slaveholders in the French and Spanish West Indies accepted the African captives as fellow human beings. They did not believe that it was necessary to insist that the African captives give up all of their customs and traditions.

African customs and traditions, especially in dance, were not really considered culture in the European way of viewing things. There was a major difference between European and African ideas of the purposes of dance. West and Central Africans shared the tradition that dance was a major part of their lives and culture, whereas white society considered dance mainly a form of entertainment. This emphasis on dance as entertainment caused Africans brought to the New World to create a combination of European and African traditions.

Some amiable plantation owners would allow the slaves to have dances. Plantation owners often used Saturday night dances as an incentive for the slaves to be more productive at work. The dances were first held on the grass outside of the shacks that housed the slaves, but eventually dance houses were built. Because the slaves had few recreational activities, the dances quickly became very popular. A lively evening of dance and song was usually accompanied by a fiddle, banjo, or tambourine.

Sometimes whites came down from the "big house" to amuse them-

When the slaves held dances, they were often accompanied by a banjo.

selves by watching the slaves dance. Africans imitated European dances, but they added elements of their own traditional dance forms. The slaves' dances reminded the whites of popular European-derived ballroom steps such as quadrilles, reels, and cotillions. The enslaved Africans probably learned these dances by watching the fancy dress balls in the "big house" where the best black fiddle players were often used to provide the music.

Some European dances were similar to African native circle dances. In America, the African version of these dances included shouting, clapping, swaying to the music, stamping of the feet, and shuffling in a counter-clockwise direction. Some dance participants would leave the circle to make up new and more complicated steps in the center. This set the stage for competitions among the slaves, which would honor and praise the best dancers. Similar types of dances still exist throughout Central and West

The traditional African circle dance was brought to America and adapted by the slaves.

Africa and among the isolated black communities of an island chain along the Atlantic coast of Georgia called the Sea Islands.

A group of dancers from Dahomey (the former name of the West African country of Benin) performed at the Chicago World's Fair in 1893. This event brought attention to the exciting movements and rhythms of African dance and showed both black and white Americans that such dancing could be artistically appealing and very entertaining.

Efforts to directly incorporate some of the features of native African dances into modern American dances did not begin until the 1930s. The

African dance styles were brought to the attention of the public in the dance drama Kykunkor.

New York production of *Kykunkor* by Asadata Dafora was the first publicly acclaimed dance drama to bring African dance styles to public attention. During the same period, the Creative Dance Institute of Hampton performed with a young Liberian dancer named Toniea Massaquoi at Radio City Music Hall. Edith Isaacs, the editor of *Theater Arts* magazine, recognized Massaquoi's ability to bring out both ancient African and modern dance forms in a way that expressed his "own free African character and sense of beauty."

Minstrel Shows and Darktown Follies

Mainstream America's acceptance of black forms of social recreation, artistic expression, and entertainment came when whites were attracted to the beauty of African-influenced movements and rhythms. White entertainers began to imitate the moves and music that they watched and heard in the slave quarters. These performances became an important part of early minstrel shows.

In a minstrel show, the performers sat in chairs arranged in a semicircle on the stage. The master of ceremonies, called the interlocutor, would present each entertainer in turn. The chorus sang the melody for the dances, often clapping their hands or using tambourines.

Blackface minstrelsy came from white entertainers who darkened their faces and imitated African-American musical and dance traditions. One of the first white entertainers to perform dances in the style of African slaves was an actor named Tea. Appearing in Philadelphia in 1767 with The American Company, Tea did "a negro dance." He took burnt cork and blackened his face so that he would look more "authentic." Other performers copied him. Minstrel shows were the most popular form of entertainment in America from the 1830s until the early twentieth century. This type of show was one result of European and African dance and musical traditions coming together.

Minstrelsy became even more popular after a white actor named Thomas Dartmouth Rice saw an elderly African-American man singing and

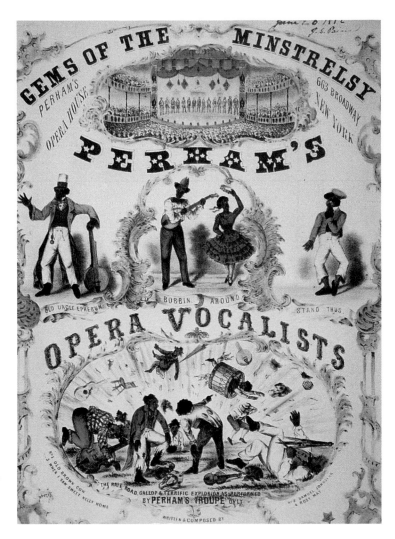

This cover for sheet music shows some of the numbers performed by minstrels in 1872.

dancing in the stable behind a theater where Rice was performing. The man had one shoulder higher than the other, and his leg was twisted. He was singing a song as he tried to dance a jig, but he could only limp. This looked funny to Rice. The man called himself Daddy Jim Crow. Rice created an act based on his imitation of Daddy Jim Crow's song and crooked jig. The show was a big hit and was soon copied by many other white entertainers in blackface who performed songs, skits, and dances. Rice changed his name to Daddy "Jim Crow" Rice.

Minstrel shows continued for many years. They also established negative stereotypes of African Americans that exist to the present day. Blackface minstrelsy portrayed African Americans as lazy, ignorant, and totally dependent on the kindness of white people for their survival. *Jim Crow* became a slang term for racial discrimination.

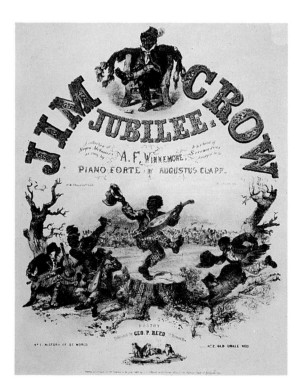

An 1847 sheet-music cover for the Jim Crow Jubilee

Black dancers were usually not allowed to perform in white minstrel shows, with the exception of a remarkable black dancer named William Henry Lane. Lane, who changed his stage name to Juba after a Haitian dance of African origin, was referred to as "Master Juba." He was regarded as one of the best dancers in the minstrel shows. In the 1840s, Lane performed in the poorer sections of New York City to audiences of African Americans and Irishmen. In 1850 he toured Europe as the star of an all-white American dance company. Europe honored him as "the greatest dancer in the world."

Minstrelsy could not have taken place without the contribution of black dance, dialect, and music. Black dancers and musicians knew that whites enjoyed their performances and began to use this appeal to their advantage. In order to make a living, however, they had to continue to portray the image of a happy-go-lucky, lazy, ignorant, and totally dependent people in their presentations to white audiences. Most whites accepted these racist stereotypes as true representations of African Americans. Whites enjoyed the "exotic" rhythms in black music and the expressive movements in black dance, although most considered it low-class entertainment.

While performing for their mostly white audiences, black entertainers constantly improvised new and original forms of dance to appeal to the growing cultural awareness of the African-American community. Social dancing proved to be an important link to their African roots.

After the Civil War, black people began performing as minstrels. The stereotypes previously presented by the white, blackfaced minstrels were so strong that black minstrels had to also wear blackface makeup and red or white lipstick to make their lips look bigger.

The first organized company of black minstrels was Lew Johnson's Plantation Minstrels, which began in the early 1860s. One of the most popular groups was the Georgia Minstrels with James Bland. Bland composed the song "Carry Me Back to Old Virginny." The Great Nonpareil Colored Troupe, the Colored Hamtown Singers, and Haverly's Mastodon

Genuine Coloured Minstrels also gave performances during that time. An integrated group called Primrose and West's Forty Whites and Thirty Blacks was formed in 1893.

Black minstrels performed almost exclusively for white audiences. Their presentations proved to be fresh and original versions of traditional minstrel routines. They also brought new techniques in dancing. The black version of Irish jig steps took the dance to another level. Other dances such as the buck and wing and the amazing stop-time dances were made popular by black minstrel groups and were early versions of the old soft shoe dances. Minstrelsy presented negative images of African Americans, but it was often the only way for a performer to appear on the popular stage.

As the 1890s were coming to a close, shows by white and black minstrels declined in popularity. Other areas began to open for African-American dancers. In 1889 a white burlesque show manager named Sam T. Jack presented an all-black production called *The Creole Show*. It was one of the first major stage productions with African-American performers. The show broke minstrel tradition by adding sixteen singing and dancing chorus girls. This was the first time that women were included in the cast. Also, unlike earlier minstrel shows, black performers did not wear blackface makeup. Other than these changes, *The Creole Show* followed the standard minstrel format. The final dance routine was called the cakewalk. It was performed by Charles Johnson and Miss Dora Dean, who remained popular entertainers until the 1930s.

The cakewalk originated among the slaves during harvesttime in the West Indies. It was once called the chalkline walk because it was a dance done by couples who followed a straight path while balancing a bucket or glass of water on their head. Dances like this were directly related to the African custom of carrying baskets, bundles, and jugs on the head.

The cakewalk was changed into a dance by African-American slaves to poke fun at the elegance and stiffness of the ballroom dances of the white plantation owners. The dance was often done in the presence of the plan-

A 1908 poster for the cakewalk

tation owner, who was amused by this entertaining and good-natured humor. *The Creole Show* revived the cakewalk and added some additional steps. Earlier forms of the cakewalk used a kind of shuffling movement, which was later changed to a smooth, walking dance step that was done with the body held erect.

The cakewalk became a popular stage act. It was performed in the early minstrel shows and was also a favorite dance of many fashionable ballrooms around the turn of the century. Several couples would form a square with the men on the inside and, while raising their feet and legs high, would strut around the square to lively ragtime music. Each couple would be eliminated one by one by several judges. Finally, the pair with the best performance was presented with a highly decorated cake.

The music for the cakewalk had a rhythm that influenced the growth of ragtime. Egbert "Bert" Williams and George Walker performed the cakewalk so well that they became one of the highest paid dance teams in the theater.

Harlem's Lafayette Theater was the stage that introduced the *Darktown Follies* in 1913. This production brought a nightly procession of whites to Harlem for entertainment. The *Darktown Follies* also introduced a new and original African-American dance that swept the country. The dance appeared in the last part of the first act and was called Ballin' the Jack.

The dance came from the plantation ring-shout, which was an American version of African circle dancing. In certain parts of West Africa, some tribes tapped out distinctive rhythms with their feet on the sun-hardened clay. This tradition proved to be a very useful device in America when the white slave owners began to outlaw the use of drums. The slaves made drum sounds with their feet on the floors of their huts or on the wooden planks of their dancing floors. This dance is usually accompanied by voices engaged in a type of chanting that builds up to several climaxes sounding like a shout.

The dance may have originally come from Moslem Arabs in northern Africa. The arabic word *saut* is similar to "shout" in English. *Saut* means to run or walk counterclockwise around the *Kaaba*, the holy Moslem shrine in Mecca. Like the Moslems, the slaves always moved in the circle in a counterclockwise direction. The dance had a circular and shuffling snake-like motion to it. Earl Tucker took the basic moves of the ring-shout, combined it with the snakelike moves of Ballin' the Jack, and it became a dance sensation. Tucker was given the nickname "Snakehips" and Ballin' the Jack soon came to be called snakehips also.

Darktown Follies was special because it broke away from the earlier minstrel traditions by adding a more serious, romantic element to the stage presentation.

FOUR

Juke Joints
to Vaudeville

African Americans in the South had to create their own forms of entertainment. Although it was discouraged by the church, most black recreational and social activity centered around dance. Segregated dance halls sprang up throughout the South. Along with them came the creation of the juke houses, or juke joints. The word *juke* meant "wicked" and was originally *dzugu* (pronounced *SHZOO goo*) from the Gullah dialect of the Bambara tribe in Africa. A juke joint was a black pleasure house where people went for dancing, drinking, and gambling. Juke joints were country versions of nightclubs.

It was in juke joints that most of the popular black dances were created. A dance always made the rounds of southern juke joints before making it to popular mainstream stages. The Black Bottom originated in a juke joint. This dance was named after a tough neighborhood in Nashville, Tennessee. The Big Apple was created in a juke joint near Columbia, South Carolina. It was rearranged by the legendary white dance school instructor Arthur Murray into a favorite ballroom selection. Other dances from juke joints of the South include the Charleston, the shimmy, and the mooche.

From 1916 to about 1930 there was a great migration of southern black Americans to the cities of the North. This was caused by years of poor crops, an increase in lynchings of black men, and the lure of jobs, especially in the defense industry during World War I. As African Americans moved around the United States, they took their dances with them.

New York's big Harlem ballrooms—the Savoy, the Renaissance, and the Alhambra—became the settings for the creation of new dances like the lindy hop, jitterbug, shag, Suzi-Q, camel walk, and truckin'. Dances created at Harlem ballrooms were used by black dancers in their acts at popular nightclubs such as the Cotton Club, Leroy's, or Small's Paradise.

The Mills Blue Rhythm Band was popular at the Cotton Club in the late 1920s.

African-American dances began moving from the nightclubs to the theaters from 1921 to 1933, a period known today as the Harlem Renaissance. There was a growing interest in presenting anything from African-American culture, especially dance. White people came to these performances expecting to be entertained with exotic dance routines and acrobatics requiring superior athletic skills. African Americans were stereotyped as naturally gifted dancers because of the so-called jungle rhythms inherited from their African ancestors.

The Harlem Renaissance was also a grand opportunity for black writers to describe to the world the exciting developments in African-American cultural expression. Writer Claude Mckay described a dance at the Congo Club as follows:

> *They danced, Rose and the boy. Oh, they danced! An exercise of rhythmical exactness for two. There was no motion she made that he did not imitate. They reared and pranced together, smacking palm against palm, working knee between knee, grinning with real joy. . . .*

Author and poet Langston Hughes wrote about the Harlem dance scene in his book *The Big Sea*:

> *The lindy-hoppers at the Savoy even began to practice acrobatic routines and to do absurd things for the entertainment of the whites, that probably never would have entered their heads to attempt merely for their own effortless amusement. Some of the lindy-hoppers had cards printed with their names on them and became dance professors teaching the tourists. Then Harlem nights became show nights. . . .*

For a while it seemed that white audiences could not get enough of these lively forms of black entertainment. From the early 1920s to the late

Dancing at the Savoy Ballroom around 1947

1930s, forty black musical shows were presented. All of them had many talented dancers and fabulous chorus lines. The precision dancing now seen in modern chorus lines was started by black dancers in these shows.

In 1921 the first and most celebrated of these performances showcasing African-American dance and music was the musical comedy *Shuffle Along*. It was written by the teams of Flournoy Miller and Aubrey Lyles, and Noble Sissle and Eubie Blake. As a production written by blacks for a black audience, it became a standard, like the blues and jazz, of what white audiences automatically attributed to blacks. The production was such a big hit that it made dancers Florence Mills and Josephine Baker overnight sensations.

Florence Mills began performing as a young girl with her sisters in a song-and-dance act called the Mills Trio. She won several awards in cake-walk and other dance competitions. After *Shuffle Along*, Mills went on to star in *Plantation Review*, *Dixie to Broadway*, and *Blackbirds*, which were all presented in 1926. Mills was also supposed to star in the production, *Blackbirds of 1928*, but she died in November of 1927.

Josephine Baker had attempted to join *Shuffle Along* at the age of fifteen, but she was too young. Baker came back when she was sixteen after she had convinced Noble Sissle and Eubie Blake that she was a spectacular talent. When Baker was given specific dance routines to follow in a chorus line, she would replace them with her own original steps. The audience thought her routines were very humorous and entertaining. Baker brought her originality to *Shuffle Along* and *Chocolate Dandies*.

Baker joined the French production of *La Revue Negre* in 1925 and became France's hot new sensation. The improvisational aspects of jazz were an important part of her dancing style, and she was responsible for France's continued interest in jazz.

The dance style of Josephine Baker popularized many of the basic elements of distinctive African dances. She created movements that imitated native African animals such as snakes and tigers.

Florence Mills was a talented performer and starred in several shows in 1926.

In 1926 Baker became one of the most popular entertainers in Europe after she appeared on stage at the Folies Bergère in Paris and performed her legendary "Banana Dance." She would not be recognized in the United States as a star until 1951, well after she had become a European legend for introducing the Charleston and the Black Bottom to audiences there.

The musical *Shuffle Along* was only the beginning of musical comedies written and produced by blacks. In 1923 Miller and Lyles wrote and produced *Runnin' Wild*. It featured and made famous a dance called the Charleston.

The Charleston was originally a black folk dance that became one of the most popular social jazz dances of the 1920s. Its movements can be traced to specific dances in the Caribbean island of Trinidad and to the Ashanti people in the West African country of Ghana. Mentioned as early as

Josephine Baker, shown here doing the cancan,
was famous for her performances at the Folies Bergères in France.

1903, the Charleston became known throughout the South. It was earlier associated with Charleston, South Carolina.

The dance was done by moving your feet with your toes in and your heels out in a series of twisting steps. In its early form the Charleston was performed to complex rhythms beaten out by foot stamps and hand claps. Professional dancers adopted the dance in 1920. After its appearance in *Runnin' Wild*, it became a national craze, but as a fashionable ballroom dance it lost some of the excitement of the earlier version.

The popular ballroom dances of the 1920s were the shimmy, the Charleston, the Black Bottom, the rumba, and the conga. All of these dances were originated or influenced by African Americans, but they were changed and refined from their original African forms so that they would be more acceptable to white Americans. Ballroom dance came from the merging of European couple dancing with African-based movements.

Musicals featuring African-American actors and dancers had a great impact on American theater and dance for many years. Just as *Runnin' Wild* made the Charleston a fashionable dance, *Shuffle Along* was responsible for making tap dancing popular during the 1920s. Tap dancing became the focal point of the various acts of the Vaudeville stage and continued to enjoy widespread appeal through the Hollywood musicals of the 1930s and 1940s.

A MASTER OF TAP DANCING

Tap dancing came from the combination of an Irish jig and an ancient African dance step called the giouba or juba. The origins of tap dancing go back to the dance styles of William Henry "Master Juba" Lane. Tap dancing came about through the cultural interchange between African Americans and Irishmen in New York City's Five Points district. Lane learned clog dancing at Irish social parties and became known as a "jig dancer." It was the incorporation of the Irish jig and the African-American version of clog dancing that eventually developed into tap dancing.

Bill "Bojangles" Robinson was born in 1878 in Richmond, Virginia, and was one of the most famous African-American dancers during the 1920s and 1930s. "Bojangles" was a name given him by childhood friends when they saw him with a tall beaver hat that belonged to a neighborhood hatmaker with the similar name of Boujasson. His first Broadway appearance was in an all-black musical by Lew Leslie called *Blackbirds of 1928*. Leslie hoped that *Blackbirds* would be as successful as *Shuffle Along* had been seven years earlier.

Bill "Bojangles" Robinson dancing with a young admirer

Robinson had developed his own version of a dance known as the stair dance, which became a standard part of his act. He tap danced up and down a flight of five steps, drawing the audience's attention to his feet by constantly watching them while he danced. Robinson brought popularity and public attention to tap dancing. He impressed white downtown audiences so much that he was established as a Broadway headliner.

Bill Robinson demonstrating his famous stair dance

A description of Robinson's style of dance is found in Marshall and Jean Stearns's book *Jazz Dance*:

> *Sandwiched between a Buck or Time Step, Robinson might use a little skating step to stop-time; or Scoot step, a crossover tap which looked like a jig; hands on hips, tapping as he went, while one foot kicked up and over the other; or a double tap, one hand on hip, one arm extended, with eyes blinking, head shaking, and derby cocked; . . . or a broken-legged or old man's dance, one leg short and wobbling with the beat; or an exit step . . .*

Robinson began a tradition of excellence in dancing that has been passed down to dancers today. Famous black dancers such as Honi Coles, Gregory Hines, and Savion Glover give Robinson credit for blazing a trail that has been followed by many other talented African-American dancers.

The connection between African dance, the African-based dances created in the juke joints, popular ballroom dances, and tap dance are closely linked to the development of modern dance. African Americans played an important part in creating exciting modern dance productions. The dance movements of Katherine Dunham and Pearl Primus brought a greater recognition to African-American dance.

SIX

TEACHING AFRICAN DANCE TRADITIONS

Katherine Dunham began dancing at an early age. Born in 1909 in Joliet, Illinois, Dunham was singing and dancing at home and in church as soon as she could walk and talk. "It was in me to dance and I had to do it to be satisfied," Dunham said. "This need for motion, for physical expression, comes to the fore. I think many parents don't want their children to dance. But it's a stronger drive than even parental pressure."

When she was a student at the University of Chicago, she attended a lecture given by a professor of anthropology. His topic was the link between African and American culture. During his lecture he mentioned that many popular dances of the day such as the lindy hop, the Black Bottom, and the cakewalk could be traced back to Africa.

Dunham began to research the topic and was excited to find books about great African kingdoms and rich and powerful civilizations with a proud cultural tradition. Dunham decided to teach African dance and opened a succession of dance studios for that purpose. Because many of the student's parents were ashamed of their African roots, they insisted that their children learn ballet. They felt that African dance was primitive, and they wanted their children to be refined.

Dunham's dance schools were failures, and she became more and more frustrated with the lack of information available to the public about African dance. She applied for and received a Rosenwald Fund grant. Dunham felt that only a dancer could properly research and understand these African-based dances.

Katherine Dunham's research on Afro-Caribbean influences on modern dance uncovered a vast African cultural heritage that goes back hundreds of years. Dunham discovered several West Indian dances that could be traced back to traditional West African ceremonies.

A number of West Indian dances with whirling movements can be traced to traditional African dances such as the one shown here.

The slave trade that supplied African labor for the sugar and cotton plantations of the Americas was the major force that brought together two groups of people from very different cultural backgrounds. The New World became the setting where European and African traditions merged to create fresh new dances of tremendous power and lasting influence.

Several West African dance traditions were kept, shared, and passed on to the next generation in parts of the South on the gulf coast and in the Caribbean. The best examples of these dance traditions are found in the former French Caribbean island colony of Haiti. Most Haitians were former West African captives who were sold to work in the sugar fields and houses of the French plantation owners.

After the French ruling class was overthrown in Haiti in 1802, many white planters fled to New Orleans, in the Louisiana territory. The trading of slaves from Haiti and other areas of the Caribbean introduced Afro-Caribbean dance to the mainland United States.

Although they were scattered throughout the Americas under the bondage of slavery, the people from Yorubaland of West Africa were especially good at preserving and adapting many of the religious practices of their ancestors. Some of these ceremonies include *sango* and *egungun* of Yorubaland in southwestern Nigeria; *candomble* of northeastern Brazil; *voudon* (voodoo) of Haiti; and *santeria* of Cuba (also found in Miami and New York). Among these different religious practices, dance is considered the way to open the door to the spirit world. Through the dance, the spirits speak and make themselves known to people. In these religions, the body is used by these spirits during certain special ceremonial dances.

In 1946 Katherine Dunham performed a West Indian-inspired dance presentation called *L'Ag Ya* (pronounced *luh AWG ya*). This dance was the fighting dance of the Caribbean island of Martinique. As brought over by West African slaves, *L'Ag Ya* was originally a wrestling match held during the Nigerian spring festival in honor of the Earth Mother. The event was a show of pride and strength. Because such feats of strength could have been

Katherine Dunham often danced accompanied by West Indian drumming.

a threat to the West Indian plantation owners, the captive Nigerians were forbidden to perform the wrestling match. To keep the tradition alive, the Nigerian captives changed it into a dance, which made it more acceptable to the plantation owners.

Much of Dunham's research is on the dances of the islands in the Caribbean. She has clearly identified the African elements in African-American dance while bringing a sense of cultural pride to African Americans. In the West Indies, many of the dances were close representations of the religious and cultural ceremonies of West Africa. In order to please the slave-holders and also to disguise their ancient African traditions, the village rituals and dance ceremonies of Martinique, Trinidad, Jamaica, Haiti, and the lesser Antilles incorporated African religious dances into Christian ceremonies. These dances were also influenced by European dances.

As both a dance pioneer and active performer, Dunham was a major influence in the development of techniques that are used in Broadway shows and by jazz dancers today. As such, she cleared the path for current and future black dancers and effectively raised public awareness of African-American dance. A New York dance reviewer said that she "put serious negro dance on the map once and for all."

The life and work of Katherine Dunham is well known in this country and throughout the world. Dunham took an active role in elevating the Western world's cultural appreciation of the beauty and power of African-American dance and its relationship to African dance traditions. She was a master teacher in the areas of dance performance as well as a scholarly researcher of the African origins of black dance in America.

Pearl Primus, like Katherine Dunham, was also interested in the African origins of dance. She had a background similar to Dunham in that she was a choreographer, anthropologist, and teacher. However, Primus's research was different from Dunham's because she focused mainly on original African dances as opposed to the modified Afro-Caribbean dance forms. Primus received a Rosenwald fellowship to study African dances. She

The dance style of Pearl Primus reflected her love for African traditional dancing.

formed her own dance company in 1944 and produced a major dance work called *African Ceremonial*. Her personal performances and major dance productions reflected the knowledge that she obtained from her travels.

Primus was born on the Caribbean island of Woodstock, Port of Spain, Trinidad, in 1919. She was a direct descendant of the Ashanti people of Africa, and her grandfather was the head dancer of Trinidad. Her mother taught her the steps to many of the dances done in Trinidad.

The family moved to New York when Primus was two years old. Her first opportunity to dance on stage came when she was in her early twenties and filled in for a lindy hopper on a program sponsored by the New Dance Group. Due to her amazingly powerful performance, she received a working scholarship at the New Dance Group. Primus studied Caribbean dance forms under Charles Weidman and LaBelle Rosette and spent hours in libraries and museums, trying to find more information on authentic African dancing. Eventually, she decided to major in anthropology and enrolled in Columbia University.

Primus felt it was important for African Americans to be exposed to their African cultural heritage and to take pride in it. She also produced several dance pieces that were reflections of African-American life in the twentieth century, including *Strange Fruit* (1945), about a woman's feelings about a lynching; *The Negro Speaks of Rivers* (1944), from a poem by Langston Hughes; and *Michael, Row Your Boat Ashore* (1979), about the bombing of churches in Birmingham, Alabama, during the 1960s.

In 1948 a generous grant from the Rosenwald Foundation enabled Primus to spend nine months studying the dances and culture of Africa. She traveled from the rain forests and grasslands of Liberia, across central Nigeria, and completed her studies in the Sudan. The Africans accepted her as a long-lost family member. In western Nigeria her name was *Omowale*, which means "child has returned home."

Upon returning to America, Primus shared the dance techniques and knowledge she'd learned about Africa in dance halls and college lecture halls. She formed a dance troupe and traveled extensively around Europe, dancing to the beat of two Afro-Haitian drummers. Primus's dancing reflected her deep appreciation of African cultural traditions. Upon returning from Africa a second time in 1960, she created a program called Meet Africa. She and her husband, Percival Borde, a Trinidadian dancer, introduced adults and New York elementary school children to the dance and culture of Africa.

Primus completed her doctoral degree in anthropology and became a college professor, a director for a performing arts center in the African country of Liberia, and a teacher of African culture.

The great love that Katherine Dunham and Pearl Primus have displayed for African-American culture has encouraged the preservation and performance of traditional African dance. Through their research and choreography, they have shown the influence of ancient African dance movements on modern dance.

SEVEN

Classical Dance

America's experience with concert-theatrical dance began with the early performances of modern dance pioneers Martha Graham, Charles Weidman, Doris Humphrey, and Helen Tamiris. African Americans were not allowed to perform with white ballet companies. The American Ballet Company formed by George Balanchine and Lincoln Kirstein in 1934 was the first one in the United States to include African Americans. In the mid-1930s several noteworthy black pioneers of modern dance, including Hemsley Winfield, Edna Guy, and Asadata Dafora, were also in the process of developing a separate and distinctive African-American dance culture.

There was limited cultural interaction between whites and blacks because of American social restrictions. In the Northeast, where most of the white audiences for black stage presentations were concentrated, African-American dancers were acceptable as long as they performed African-based material. Ballet was considered a prestigious and highly developed classical European art form. White society did not believe that blacks had the "ideal" body type or the ability to perform ballet with the

Asadata Dafora (right) *with some members of his folk dancing group.*
Dafora came to New York from Africa to present the dances of Africa.

grace, sophistication, and style that it demanded. These same attitudes also barred many African Americans from participating in modern dance troupes. African-American dancers were frequently overlooked by white choreographers.

Following World War II, few black people could receive ballet training because of the many obstacles they had to overcome to be accepted. Classical ballet instruction has to begin at a young age. It requires expensive lessons, usually from foreign teachers, which most African-American families could not afford.

Hemsley Winfield choreographed and performed in *The Emperor Jones* in 1933. Although Winfield's performance was excellent, he caused much controversy. White people were having a hard time accepting the fact that black dancers could perform classical European ballet.

When *The Emperor Jones* was presented, John Martin, a drama critic for the *New York Times*, wrote that ". . . Negroes cannot be expected to do dances designed for another race." Similar reactions rooted in racist ideas reflected extreme white prejudice in this area. Blacks were expected to perform their own dances. This idea was justified by some people who said that formal, classical dance training was harmful to blacks because it would destroy their originality and gifts of improvisation. Whites gave credit to blacks as being naturally gifted dancers, but they felt that African-based dances did not require training.

Eugene Von Grona was a German who was trained in modern dance. He studied black dances and did not understand why African Americans could not dance classical European steps. He believed that any race of people could dance well with the proper training. Von Grona ran an advertisement in a Harlem newspaper in 1934 offering free dance training to talented dancers. One hundred and fifty-eight people answered his ad, from which he selected twenty-two students over a three-year period. He called his group the First American Negro Ballet.

The first performance took place on November 12, 1937, at the

Lafayette Theater in Harlem. Their performance was well received by some and ridiculed by others. The group made a few other appearances and was disbanded in 1939 due to lack of bookings or sponsorship. Although short-lived, Von Grona's First American Negro Ballet is important because of the barrier it broke for blacks in the field of classical ballet.

As training opportunities for other kinds of dance slowly grew, blacks began to be recruited for modern dance companies. For years, however, American ballet companies would not hire black dancers.

Arthur Mitchell understood the problems of limited opportunities for blacks in classical ballet. He believed that the lack of black dancers in ballet was because "there aren't that many Negroes trained in the classics. It's not a matter of my being an exception; it's a matter of my having had more opportunities and being exposed to more."

In 1955 Mitchell was the first African American to be offered a dance position with the New York City Ballet. He was one of the first dancers to successfully bridge the historical gap between traditional classical European ballet and African-American dance culture.

In 1965 *New York Times* arts writer Allen Hughes described Mitchell as an artist who dances "without regard for color." Hughes also said of Mitchell:

> *As a principal dancer and longtime member of the New York City Ballet, he is a star of international reputation in . . . classical ballet. He is the first Negro to have attained that distinction.*

The lack of opportunities for African-American classical dancers was definitely not due to a scarcity of talent, as Hughes went on to say:

> *Mr. Mitchell is not, of course, the first or only great Negro dance artist, nor even the first to venture successfully into the classical ballet field. To date, however, he has been the only Negro to establish*

himself as a leading dancer of one of the world's great ballet compa-
nies. . . . He won his place in the New York City Ballet because he is
a superior dancer, and the company has used him freely in its reper-
tory without regard for the color of his skin.

Hughes's praise for Mitchell did not take into account the fact that Mitchell's situation was far from ideal. Although he had been a leading dancer for years, Mitchell's opportunities were still limited because of his color. As late as 1965, Mitchell was barred from performing a dance with a white ballerina on national television, even though he had done so numerous times on stages throughout the world. Hughes was quoted as saying that this restriction was because

television stations in the South would refuse to carry the shows, and
advertisers would not like that. This means quite simply that a prej-
udiced minority in this country has dictatorial power over what all
Americans will be allowed to see.

Arthur Mitchell led the way for black dancers who wanted to find opportunities to perform in classical dance. He once said, "I believe in helping people the best way you can, my way is through my art. But sometimes you need a splash of cold water in your face to make you see the right way to do it."

The "cold water" Mitchell was referring to was the assassination of Martin Luther King, Jr. The incident moved him so much that he founded a school called the Dance Theater of Harlem (DTH). The purpose of the school was "to promote interest in and teach young people the art of classical ballet, modern and ethnic dance, thereby creating a much needed self-awareness and better self-image of the students themselves," Mitchell said.

Mitchell eventually wanted to develop a performing company made up of highly disciplined and technically trained dancers from the school. He

*In this 1973 photo Arthur Mitchell (center) is surrounded
by twenty-three dancers from his Dance Theater of Harlem.*

boldly stated: "We have to prove that a black ballet school and a black ballet company are the equal of the best of their kind, anywhere in the world."

The Dance Theater of Harlem has definitely secured its place in dance history. In 1985 Mitchell described the success of his school and company as follows:

> . . . *with the acceptance of DTH and the popularity of the company not only here in America but around the world, progress definitely has been made. It may not be as fast or as complete as one would like, but there's no question and no doubt in anyone's mind now about black dancers doing classical ballet.*

EIGHT

TRIUMPHS IN BALLET

After 1970 critics slowly began to change their minds about African Americans and classical ballet after seeing the performances of Arthur Mitchell, Carmen de Lavallade, Janet Collins, Geoffrey Holder, Alvin Ailey, Judith Jamison, and several highly skilled African-American dance companies.

Janet Collins, a Louisiana native, moved to California as a child during the late 1920s with her family. She first received notoriety as a major participant in the first tour of Katherine Dunham's Dance Troupe. In 1947 she electrified audiences with a solo performance at the Las Palmas Theater in Los Angeles. From her West Coast success she leaped onto the East Coast stages, making her New York City debut in 1949. Collins went from the lead dancer in Cole Porter's Broadway musical *Out of This World* to become the prima ballerina of the world famous Corps de Ballet of the Metropolitan Opera of New York in 1951.

Janet Collins's cousin, Carmen de Lavallade, was also taking the classical dance scene by storm. In 1966 *Dance Magazine* described de Lavallade as a "beauteous symbol of today's total dancer, she conveys the sensuous pleasure of movement with simplicity, elegance and superb control."

Janet Collins dancing in the opera Aida

Carmen de Lavallade was the principle dancer for the Lester Horton Dance Theater where she performed in *House of Flowers* on Broadway in 1954. She was honored by art critic Doris Hering as a "star in the most luxuriant sense of the word," and by *New York Herald Tribune* arts writer Walter Terry as "a vision of loveliness." She made guest appearances with the dance companies of Geoffrey Holder (who is her husband), Donald McKayle, John Butler, Glen Tetley, and Alvin Ailey and was the prima ballerina of New York City Opera, the American Ballet Theater, and the Boston Ballet.

Walter Terry describes de Lavallade as follows:

> *Watching Miss de Lavallade move—with flowing gestures of arms and fingers or taking an arabesque-like stance in lyrical slow motion or cutting the air with eager leaps—one never thinks about choreography, whether it is good or bad, for Miss de Lavallade seems to transcend mere form as she gives us the very radiance, subdued or brightly shining, of dance itself.*

Carmen de Lavallade has had a stellar career that includes her work as a choreographer, actress, teacher, and humanitarian. She is proud of her African heritage. Speaking on the contributions of black dancers to dance in America, she once stated " . . . when given a chance to create and develop, [black dancers] will give joy and beauty to the world. . . . Dance is dance, music is music, art is art, let us all enjoy it together."

Geoffrey Holder, a native of Port of Spain, Trinidad, inherited his brother Boscoe's dance company before making a name for himself in the United States. His Broadway debut came in 1954 in Truman Capote's *House of Flowers*. Holder became a leading dancer of the Metropolitan Opera Ballet in 1956.

Regarding Geoffrey Holder, Allyn Moss wrote in an article for the August 1956 issue of *Dance Magazine*:

To anyone who has ever watched this restless young man dance there is no need to describe the impact his long dark body, suggestive of Egyptian tribal kings, makes as it twists around a rhythm seemingly unrestricted by the usual bonds of bone and muscle, or struts . . . against the rhythm of a drum.

Holder has strong feelings about the attitudes of African-American dancers and how their audiences have treated them in the United States. Race should not be an issue as far as Holder is concerned. He says:

People worry about the wrong things. This gets in the way of creativity. When I paint, I paint. I'm not a Negro painter. When I dance, I dance. I'm not a West Indian dancer. I'm not a voodoo dancer, not a ballet dancer—I'm a dancer.

Holder has not only been a dancer, but also a director, actor, painter, costume designer, and choreographer. Holder has choreographed works for the Boston Ballet, the Dance Theater of Harlem, and the Alvin Ailey Dance Theater.

Alvin Ailey's life-long interest in classical dance was sparked by a field trip. In junior high school Alvin Ailey and his class attended the Ballet Russe de Monte Carlo. From that day on, he knew he wanted to be a dancer. Ailey was originally from Texas but moved to California at the age of twelve. Much of his inspiration came from the performances of the Katherine Dunham Dance Company.

Ailey began his formal dance training with Lester Horton, who had one of the first racially integrated dance companies in California. When Horton died, Ailey became the director of the Lester Horton Dance Theater, where he was the choreographer of several original works. He was a friend of Carmen de Lavallade and travelled with her to New York to dance in *House of Flowers*.

Alvin Ailey, Ella Thompson Moore, and Myrna White in
Revelations, *a modern dance classic choreographed by Ailey*

In 1954 Ailey had the opportunity to study with Martha Graham, Doris Humphrey, and Charles Weidman, who were some of the most outstanding dance artists of that time. He also established a reputation as a fine stage actor.

Ailey formed his own company in 1958. The Alvin Ailey Dance Theater (AADT) was Ailey's vision of a dance company that was committed to the enrichment and preservation of black cultural traditions by means of modern American dance. Ailey choreographed *Revelations* in 1960, a modern dance based on the religious heritage of blacks in America. It became a classic masterpiece of modern dance.

Ailey has been a giant among all of the leaders of African-American cultural development. He personally created 79 ballets. Ailey enjoyed using the work of other choreographers and staging revivals of works created by Katherine Dunham, Pearl Primus, Talley Beatty, and other African-American dancers. The AADT performed 170 works by sixty-three choreographers.

In 1965 he discovered an incredibly gifted dancer named Judith Jamison. Jamison's brilliant dance style inspired Ailey to use her in a solo dance presentation *Cry*, which was a tribute to his mother, Mrs. Lula E. Cooper, and African-American women everywhere. Jamison's premiere performance created such a sensation that *Cry* has been described as "one of the great moments in American dance."

Ailey's ballets are performed by many of the world's best dance companies including the American Ballet Theater, Joffrey Ballet, Paris Opera Ballet, La Scala Ballet, and Dance Theater of Harlem. The Ailey Camp, a dance school for children, was formed as a result of AADT's commitment to arts education programs. Ailey received numerous awards and wide recognition for his achievements. He died on December 1, 1989. Other dancers like Judith Jamison continue to carry on his commitment to African-American dance tradition.

Jamison was originally from Philadelphia, where she began dancing at

Alvin Ailey danced with Hope Clark in this 1978 performance of his Blues Suite. *This was one of his last performances on stage.*

the age of six at the Judimar School of Dance. She attended Fisk University in Tennessee on a physical education scholarship and majored in psychology. She left after three semesters to pursue a career in dance. She enrolled at the Philadelphia Dance Academy, where she studied ballet and modern dance.

Jamison was discovered by the great choreographer Agnes de Mille, who helped her make her New York City debut with the American Ballet Theater. When the ABT released Jamison from her contract, she faced a problem securing another position as a dancer. She felt that she wouldn't have as much trouble if her arms weren't so long, if she wasn't so tall (five foot eleven inches), athletically built, and dark-skinned. She had almost decided to return to Philadelphia when she came to the attention of Alvin Ailey, who recruited her for the AADT. Jamison was a great success with the company and performed some of Ailey's best-known ballets. Her dancing took her all over the world.

Jamison left AADT to appear in the musical *Sophisticated Ladies* in 1980. She founded her own dance company, the Jamison Project, in 1988 and later merged it with the AADT. When Ailey died in 1989, she was appointed Artistic Director of AADT, a position she still holds.

Judith Jamison describes herself as " . . . a dancer who happens to be a woman who happens to be black." She is one of the most influential voices in modern dance today. As artistic director of the Alvin Ailey Dance Theater, she is a mentor to hundreds and an inspiration to thousands of African-American men and women who desire to become professional dancers.

New generations of classically trained dancers are continuing to explore their African roots through modern dance.

One of them is Jeraldyne Blunden, founder of the Dayton Contemporary Dance Company. Blunden began training as a dancer at age five with Josephine and Hermine Schwarz in Dayton, Ohio. Because of racial segregation, Blunden was forced to study ballet in a separate class from the

Judith Jamison starred in Cry, *Alvin Ailey's tribute
to his mother and to all African-American women.*

white students. "It wasn't so much Miss Jo and Miss Hermine as the parents [of the other students]," Blunden says. She continued dancing through college, marriage, and motherhood, and began teaching and choreographing dances for her talented students. She formally established the Dayton Contemporary Dance Company in 1968.

In 1976 the Company performed a dance called *Black Show* and began to attract the attention of audiences around the United States, as well as famous choreographers such as Talley Beatty, Donald McKayle, and Eleo Pomare. The Company became one of the first African-American dance companies in the nation to acquire a piece by choreographer Merce Cunningham when they began performing his work *Channel Inserts*.

"You could call what I do black dance because I'm a black dance person," says Blunden. "What I do is from a black perspective. But people who are sure of themselves don't bother with that."

Another classically trained modern dancer is Kevin Jeff, founder of the Jeff's Jubilation! Dance Company. The company mixes jazz, modern, ballet, and traditional African dance to create exciting movements such as an African head roll combined with a classical arabesque.

"The African movement is the glue that links together the ballet, modern, and jazz," Jeff once said. "It's dynamic and healing. It requires a lot of stamina, but it's subtle. It has a lot of impact as theater."

With the new awareness of the role that African culture has on American dance and the stellar performances presented by African-American ballet dancers, classical dance has moved into the modern age.

NINE

A New Age for African-American Dance

Public or street dancing is a natural component of West African dance culture. Dancers Honi Coles and James "Buster" Brown both began their careers dancing in public and giving street performances.

The popular dances of the 1970s and 1980s borrowed much of their movement and rhythms from Africa. In the 1970s, disco dancing blended the pulsing, funky beat of soul music with the smooth tempo and syncopated rhythms of Latin dance music. John Travolta became an icon for this age with his disco performance in the movie *Saturday Night Fever*. Disco was similar in many ways to earlier ballroom dancing, but it was much faster. Disco was influenced by the Latin samba but also had sophisticated acrobatic movements.

The trend toward adding more complicated movements to public social dance routines contributed to the creation of "break dancing" in the 1980s. This type of dancing began on the streets of Harlem and the South Bronx. Break dancing required an almost gymnastic level of physical ability and became popular with professional choreographers for movies and

Break dancing developed on the streets of New York City and spread to other major cities such as Los Angeles.

music videos. Soon break dancing became a major cultural development in popular dance. Modern tap dancers like Savion Glover have used break-dancing steps in their performances.

The New York City ghettos were where the roots of break dancing branched out into a separate "hip-hop" culture. The African tradition of public dancing as a means of establishing one's position in the tribe was readily transplanted to ghetto youths' dance competitions to show their athletic abilities and sense of style.

"I think break dancing grew out of a need on the part of street youth to express themselves physically," Katherine Dunham once said. "It's almost like overcoming gravity, overcoming all of the obstacles. You don't just turn twelve times like Nureyev, you turn twenty-four times."

The term *break dancing* is said to have come out of an effort by a black disc jockey named Afrika Bambaataa to diffuse tension between violent inner-city gangs. In 1969 he presented an idea to several rival gang members. He suggested that there could be a "break" in their street war if they would fight by competing with dance steps instead of physical confrontations.

Break dancing was closely associated with the highly rhythmic and rhyming style of rap music. When disc jockeys began to experiment with two or more turntables and use electronic synthesizers to make new sounds, a whole new area of music opened. The sound they produced was blasted through portable "boom boxes" giving street dancing a whole new meaning.

As one of the most popular entertainers of the twentieth century, Michael Jackson has also had a major influence on current dance styles. Jackson popularized dances such as the "robot," the "moonwalk," and the "electric boogie," which came out of the break dance tradition.

When Jackson released his video for the song "Beat It" from his *Thriller* album, a new dance step called the "worm" was created by Michael Peters, a Tony award-winning choreographer. The dance routines in today's music videos have become so important that they have elevated the status of choreographers like Peters and opened doors for African-American choreographers like Debbie Allen.

As a major performer in modern dance, Debbie Allen has achieved success as a talented choreographer, as well as an actress and producer. Inspired by a performance of Alvin Ailey's *Revelations*, she began taking dance lessons at the age of three. Allen, like many aspiring African-American dancers, had to overcome racial discrimination before she could become a successful entertainer.

Allen went on to become a star in several television and Broadway stage productions. As a choreographer, Allen coordinated the dance sessions for many stage and screen productions such as *The Cosby Show*, *A Different World*, and the 1995 Academy Awards. She has been honored with many awards including a Tony nomination for her role as a singer, actress, and dancer in *West Side Story* and an Emmy for her choreography in the television series based on the movie *Fame*.

Like Debbie Allen, Gregory Hines also was interested in dance at an early age. Hines, however, started performing tap dancing routines at local talent shows at the age of five along with his brother Maurice, and they made their debut at the Apollo Theater as the Hines Kids the next year. He soon met the famous choreographer Henri LeTang. LeTang was the best tap-dance coach for Broadway dancers at that time and was instrumental in helping Gregory and Maurice to become world famous tap dancers.

Debbie Allen in the television series Fame

Gregory Hines is famous for his tap dancing. He appeared as Sandman Sims in The Cotton Club, *a film about the legendary Harlem jazz-age nightclub.*

A revival in tap dancing came in 1978 with the theater production of *Eubie*, which was a musical tribute to the music of Eubie Blake. Both Hines brothers had parts in the musical. Gregory's energetic performance earned him a Tony nomination and an Outer Critic's Circle Award. In 1980 Gregory Hines also did the choreography for an off-Broadway show called *Blues in the Night*. That same year he appeared in another tribute called *Black Broadway*, which honored past black Broadway musicals.

Black Broadway brought public acclaim to two little-known but important figures in tap dance history, Honi Coles and John Bubbles (who starred in the Buck and Bubbles tap-dance team). Gregory Hines also starred in *Sophisticated Ladies* with Judith Jamison, which was directed and choreographed by Donald McKayle. Henri LeTang choreographed the tap-dance scenes. Hines is probably best remembered for his role as the famous tap dancer Sandman Sims in *The Cotton Club*, his costarring role with international ballet great Mikhail Baryshnikov in the movie *White Nights*, and his fabulous routines with Sammy Davis, Jr. and talented new tap dancer Savion Glover in *Tap* and *Jelly's Last Jam*.

Savion Glover is a recent tap-dance phenomenon. This twenty-one-year-old dance prodigy has elevated tap dancing to a new level. Savion captivates his audiences by the sheer power of his creative delivery and fresh new style. Watching Savion tap dance shows the potential for tap becoming as fine a dance art as classical European ballet.

Savion is one of the youngest men in dance history to be nominated for a Tony Award for his role in *Black and Blue*. At the age of twelve, he played the title character in *The Tap Dance Kid*. He has made numerous television appearances for PBS, Nickelodian, the Academy Awards, and Black Filmmakers Hall of Fame.

Savion has danced on the best concert stages in the world including Carnegie Hall, Lincoln Center, and the Moulin Rouge in France. He received an endowment grant for choreography from the NEA, making him one of the youngest people in history to receive this honor. His regular appearances on the children's television program *Sesame Street* have helped to introduce the age-old art of tap dancing to a new young audience.

His recent production of the Broadway musical *Bring In Da Noise, Bring In Da Funk,* is a combination of several different aspects of African-American dance and music. The numerous awards the production has received is evidence that the African-influenced art of tap dancing is back in style and is a tribute to the talent and ingenuity of Savion Glover.

African and African-American dance traditions have been interwoven into every phase of modern dance from classical ballet to hip-hop. African-American dancers continue to create new and exciting steps and dance styles. Most modern dance troupes are not limited to classical European ballet or Afro-centric styles of dance, and they often explore many areas of dance expression in their performances.

The award-winning Dimensions Dance Theater was cofounded by Deborah Vaughan, who is also its artistic director. Vaughan has said that she always felt that dance was more than just an outlet for self-expression. Her dance experiences began in the 1960s when dance pioneer Ruth Beckford introduced her to African dance. Vaughan's passionate interest in African-American history inspired her to use dance as a means to explore larger social issues.

Vaughan has a broad and extensive background in dance, having studied modern dance, ballet, and jazz with master teachers Louis Alley, Tally Beatty, and Alvin Ailey. In 1972 Vaughan was preparing to submit her master's thesis in dance at Mills College. She and fellow graduate student Eleander Barnes choreographed a dance piece for some local high school students, which later became the basis for the Dimensions Dance Theater.

The group's popularity has increased over the years, attracting such diverse and famous artists as South African trumpet player Hugh Masekela, jazz guitarist Stanley Jordan, and the Hawkins Family gospel singers.

Dimensions Dance Theater has stayed on the cutting edge by using

Savion Glover, today's tap-dancing sensation, in a 1995 performance

dance as a vehicle to dramatize relevant slices of life that are reflective of modern urban society. A Los Angeles rap group, The College Boyz, worked together with Dimensions to present a "choreodrama" about a young black man who was wounded in a drive-by shooting. In the presentation he discovers his ancestors, who use dance as a path to liberation.

Vaughan's multimedia presentation called *Project Panther* about the Black Panther Party, combines dance, videos, and movie clips. Vaughan worked with former Panther David Hilliard and Fredricka Newton, who was Panther founder Huey Newton's widow. Vaughan's goal is to use the production to educate people on the positive aspects of the Black Panther movement. Vaughan says that, "I've never had the luxury of simply doing dance for dance's sake. I use dance the way people use dance in Africa—for a purpose."

Another modern dancer and choreographer who promotes the African influence is Bill T. Jones. Jones has become a leader in fusing the work of famous African-American musicians and writers. He has said, "I knew that I could say things by performing. I was expressing myself. I loved the idea of moving art."

Jones's work often deals with modern social themes as well as traditional African and African-American dance forms. In 1982 he and Arnie Zane formed the Bill T. Jones/Arnie Zane Dance Company. The premiere of *Intuitive Momentum* with drummer Max Roach gave the company international recognition. Roach uses many African instruments as part of his performances. Together, he and Jones proved to be a powerful force.

Jones's *The Last Supper at Uncle Tom's Cabin/The Promised Land* is a performance piece based on Harriet Beecher Stowe's 1852 novel about the horrors of slavery. The work combines minstrel-show dancing, modern dance, gospel singing, and a cast of fifty dancers and actors.

African-American dancer and choreographer Ralph Lemon, like Jones, refuses to be bound by race, but he realizes that his heritage is rooted in African dance. After seeing a performance by Le Vaughn Robinson, a street corner tap dancer, Lemon created *Buck Dance*. The work is based on the clog dancing done by slaves. Lemon has said, "Part of us wants to be black and rooted in black tradition. Another part of us wants to be free. It all creates a wonderful tension for the work."

The Harlem Nutcracker is a recent work developed by choreographer Donald Byrd. Byrd took the classical ballet *The Nutcracker* by Tchaikovsky and transformed it into a uniquely African-American-inspired presentation. The original idea and jazzy score were created more than thirty years ago by musicians Duke Ellington and Billy Strayhorn. Composer David Berger lengthened the musical score and Byrd created the dances.

The Harlem Nutcracker uses a Harlem nightclub setting, fashionable clothes, and dances ranging from the jitterbug to modern hip-hop to give the historic ballet a definite African-American flavor. In this production, an elderly widow named Clara fights off the Angel of Death with the help of a nutcracker that was a gift from her husband. He appears as a ghost to take her through scenes of their life together, including the swinging 1930s, the civil rights movement, and the joys and sorrows of her present life. *The Harlem Nutcracker* provides a look at the bonds of modern African-American family life that is seldom seen as part of a ballet.

The development and changes in African-American dance traditions are almost parallel to the changing relationships throughout history between African Americans and American society. Slavery and racial segregation greatly affected the formation of modern African-American dance styles. From colonial times to the middle of this century, African Americans were usually kept out of the mainstream of American political, social, and economic life. If there was any benefit from this segregation, it was that it forced black people to develop new ways of expressing themselves culturally, as a displaced people having to survive in a separate society. Major elements of African-American dance have been routinely taken by whites and

A scene from the 1996 production of The Harlem Nutcracker

incorporated into their culture, usually without showing appreciation for or giving any credit to the source.

Since ancient times, dance has played a major role in the culture and society of Africa and in the lives of African Americans. Dance represented a physical expression of creativity that was tightly woven into the fabric of African life, and it became a way of dealing with the repressions and triumphs of life in America. The African's love of dance survived through the middle passage and the hardships of life in the New World. Dance was a powerful way to express the story of everyday life and became a bridge between Africa and America.

FURTHER READING

Gates, Henry Louis. *African-American Voices of Triumph: Creative Fire.* Alexandria, Virg.: Time-Life Books, 1994.

Haskins, James. *Black Dance in America: A History Through Its People.* New York: Harper Collins, 1990.

Haskins, Jim. *The Harlem Renaissance.* Brookfield, Conn.: The Millbrook Press, 1996.

Hughes, Langston and Milton Meltzer. *Black Magic: A Pictorial History of the African-American in the Performing Arts.* New York: Da Capo Press, 1967.

Westridge Young Writer's Workshop. *Kids Explore America's African American Heritage.* Santa Fe, N.M.: John Muir Publications Inc., 1993.

FOR OLDER READERS

Barthel, Joan. "When You Dream, Dream Big." *New York Times* (August 18, 1968), 22.

DiLorenzo, Kris. "Dance" *The Crisis* (June/July, 1985), 46.

Emery, Lynne Fauley. *Black Dance From 1619 to Today*. Princeton, N.J.: Princeton Publishing, 1988.

Ghent, Henri. "Dance Theatre of Harlem: A Study of Triumph Over Adversity." *The Crisis* (June, 1980), 201.

Hazzard-Gordon, Katrina. *Jookin', the Rise of Social Dance Formations in African-American Culture*. Philadelphia: Temple University Press, 1990.

Potter, Joan and Constance Claytor. *African-American Firsts: Famous, Little-Known, & Unsung Triumphs of Blacks in America*. Elizabethtown, N.Y.: Pinto Press, 1994.

Van Collie, Shimon-Craig. "Dancing with a Purpose." *Essence* (February, 1996), 60.

INDEX